The Panda,
the Cat
and the
Dreadful
Teddy

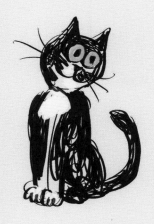

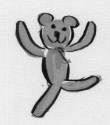

Paul Magrs

---

*

(It's a
<u>silent</u>
`g` !!)

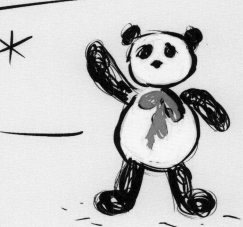

HarperCollins*Publishers*
1 London Bridge Street
London SE1 9GF

www.harpercollins.co.uk

HarperCollins*Publishers*
1st Floor, Watermarque Building,
Ringsend Road, Dublin 4, Ireland

First published by HarperCollins*Publishers* 2021

10 9 8 7 6 5 4 3 2 1

© Paul Magrs 2021

Paul Magrs asserts the moral right to be identified
as the author of this work

A catalogue record of this book is available from
the British Library

ISBN 978-0-00-849115-4

Printed and bound in Latvia

MIX
Paper from
responsible sources
FSC™ C007454

This book is produced from independently
certified FSC™ paper to ensure responsible
forest management.

For more information visit:
www.harpercollins.co.uk/green

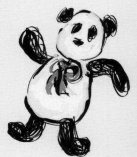

for Jeremy

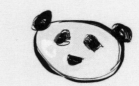

Hello!

Well done! Thank you so _so_ much for buying my book! Out of all the books in the world you chose _mine_! I'm _so_ pleased.

Gosh, it's so hard to concentrate just now, isn't it? With the world how it is and everything. I hope my book can help you. Look at all the lovely pictures!

I'm Panda, and this book is all about me and my lovely friends, all of us living our best lives and learning to be kind to one another. That's what it's all about, isn't it?

I think the whole point of making books is to make the world a better place. I'm here to lighten your load just a little bit. And so is the Cat. The Cat's quite nice. He can be a bit selfish some times, I suppose.

Then there's Teddy too.
He can come across as very nice,
with his squeaky voice and
looking so tiny and helpless.
But I must warn you. Teddy
can be a vicious little backstabber,
actually. I'm not kidding,
either. Plus, he's only
gone and got himself
his own book deal off
the back of appearing in this
one.

But never mind. We must
always try to be forgiving and kind,
and remember that life is a
great big journey into a whole
book filled with mostly blank pages.

Really, in the end, I think a book like this one is something like a lovely big hug. Yes, I do — a really lovely warm hug from someone you actually care about. And isn't a hug what we all really, really need?

So here's a lovely hug from me to all of you.

Not Teddy, though. He can go and fuck himself.

"That's the little arsehole I'm trying to *avoid*!"

"I'm the cat!"

"Hello."

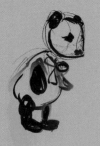

"oh shit, it's
that awful
Teddy..."

"I'm tiny," said Teddy. "But I'm still so important."

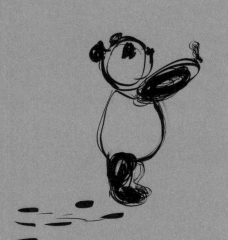

"are you bollocks," Panda told him.

"Hello, ladies!"

"Teddy told me that life is a kind of journey..."

"Ugh".

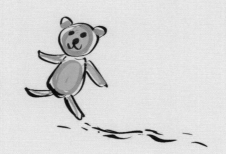

"Remember, Panda —
you are important
and you are
loved."

"Moron."

"I find that Teddy is full of tolerance and empathy," says the Cat.

"Oh?" says Panda.

"I find he's full of shit."

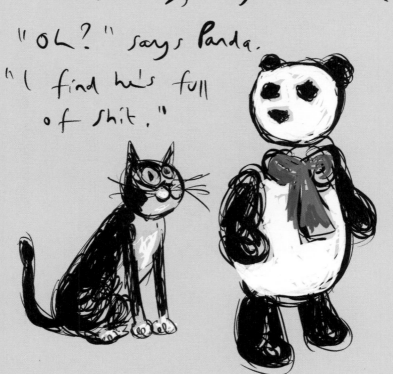

"Be more Panda!" said Panda.

"If you don't blow your own trumpet, no other fucker will."

"Shitty weather
again."

"We're just so, so lucky to have each other as friends," said Teddy.

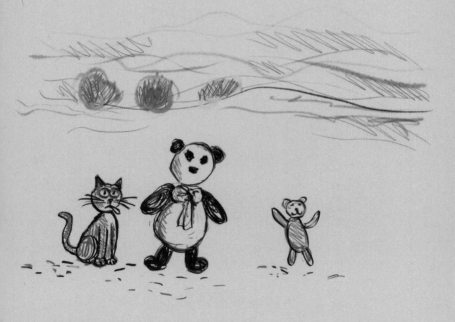

"and it's going to make a marvellous book."

"Life is like a roller coaster" says Teddy.

Panda loudly wonders whether that bear will ever know how banal he is.

Look how

Special we are.

"Panda...?"

"Yes, Cat?"

"Teddy says that he sometimes feels so hopelessly confused and tiny."

"He needs to get a fucking grip," says Panda.

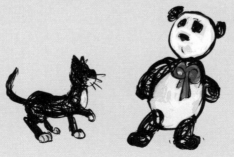

"Shit.
I can't get
down.
fuck.
Help...!"

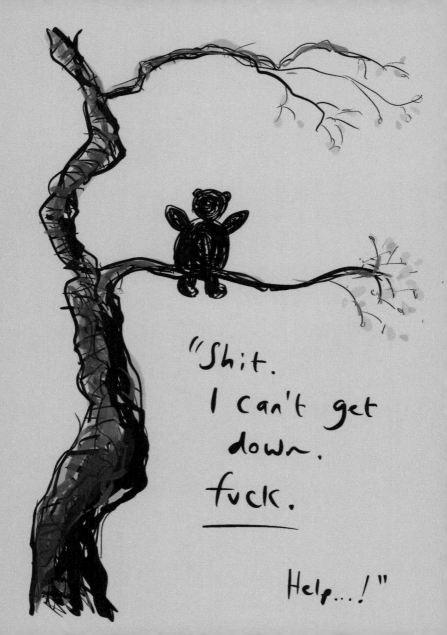

"Today it's "International Don't listen to absolute fuckers Talking Complete Shite Day'," said Panda.

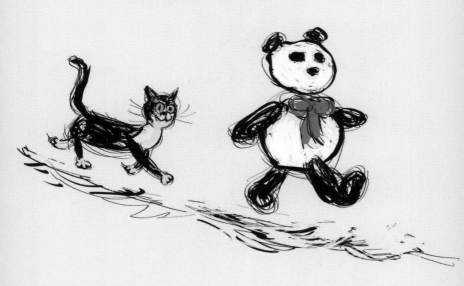

"No thanks...

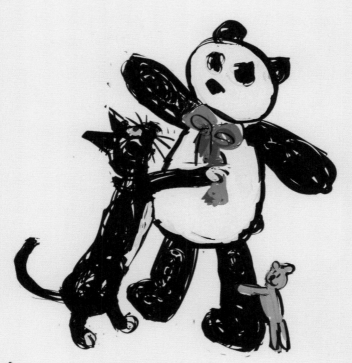

I don't actually want
a hug from you today."

"It's Motivational Monday, Panda...!"

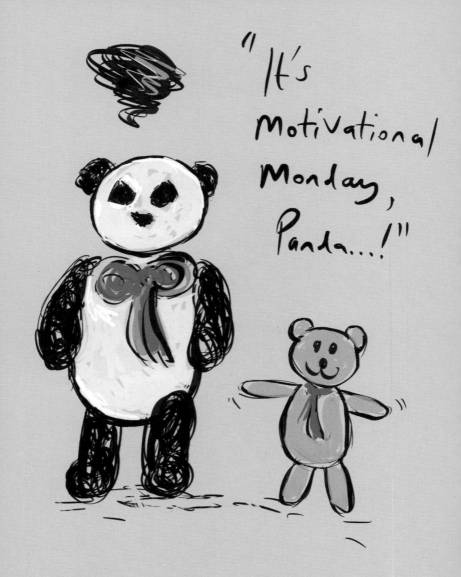

"If you don't stop saying inspirational things to me," said Panda, "I am going to punch you up the hooter."

"Cat's quiet...?"

"Existential crisis. all Cats get them"

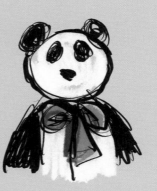

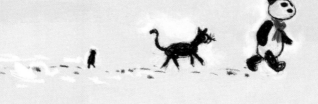

"Bloody long
winter, this..."

"You
haven't got

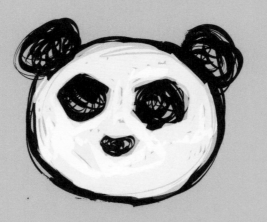

a fucking
clue."

"Teddy, I'm so glad you feel that you're `Winning at life.' Well done you, Now piss off."

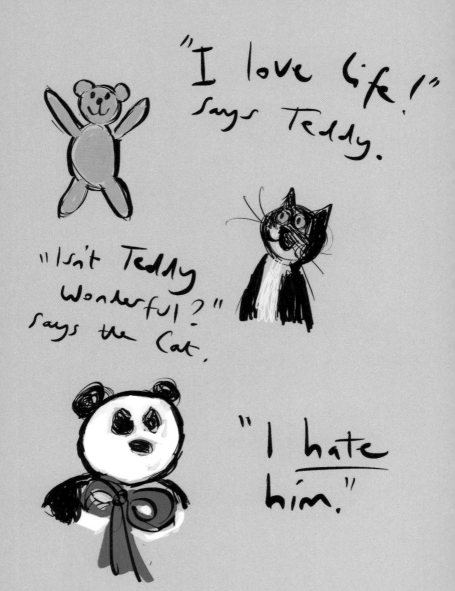

"I love life!"
says Teddy.

"Isn't Teddy
Wonderful?"
says the Cat.

"I hate
him."

"It's so important to make time for the things you are passionate about," says Teddy.

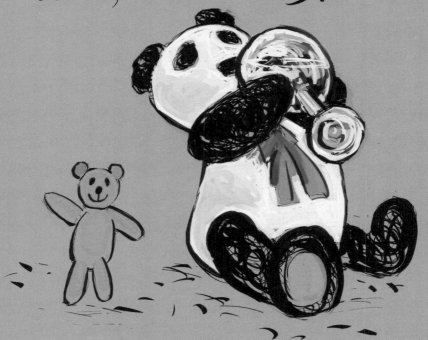

"Why not practise your mindfulness by colouring in this picture of Panda and the Cat in a snowy field...?"

"Because it's all black and white, you absolute bell-end."

"art is for everyone!" says Panda. "Unless you're completely shit at it."

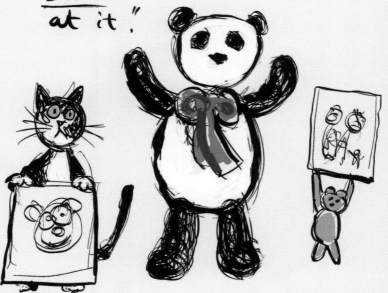

"like the Cat and Teddy are."

Weee-ooo!!

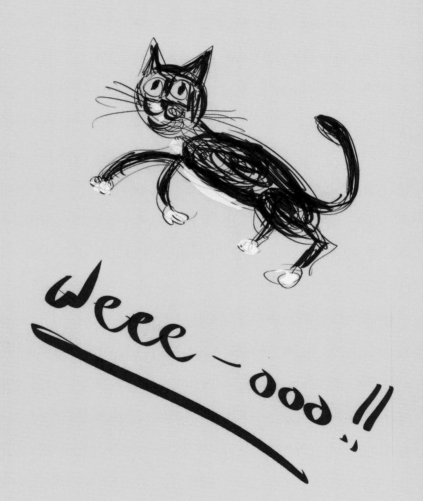

"a lovely picnic
in the countryside
and there's no
sign...
... of that bastard
Teddy."

"fuck off, Teddy — I'm reading."

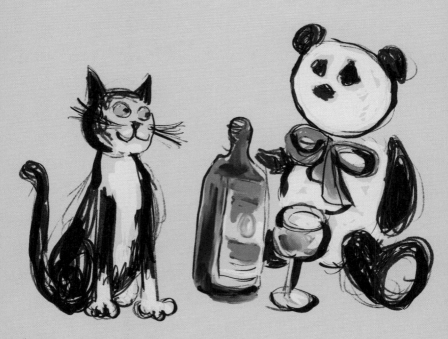

"Is your glass half empty,
or...?"
"Just give me the bottle,
you tit."

"Everyone is just so special."
"Yes, but some of them are absolute fuckers."

"I told Teddy that he should write down all his rubbishy thoughts and then publish them in a book. Now he is. Some people really don't get sarcasm, do they, Cat —?"

Mow?

"at the end of the day I just want to be a better person," says Teddy.
"I'm already fucking fabulous," says Panda.

Arse and Wank and fuck
and Bollocks
tit-ends
fuckshit farty bum
piss-face holes
UP YOURS
Twat sod
fanny fart
mollocking
crusties
fudgeknocking
fimble
famble
arselicking
shit-stirring
fuckwit

"Do you think Panda has a problem with his anger...?"
"No, he just loves to swear."

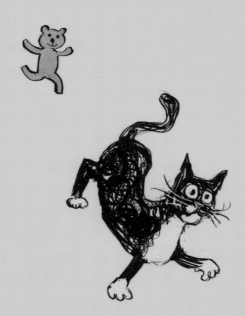

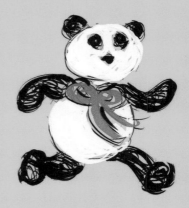

"I hope we never get too grown up to run around and go on daft."

"But Panda," said Teddy.
"Don't you ever feel you should be somewhere else doing something more useful and important?"
"Nope. Never."

"Don't you feel that we're making beautiful new memories every single day?"
"No, fuck that shit," says Panda.

"Live, laugh, Love!"
"Eat, shit, die."

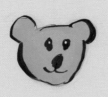

"I feel
hopeful."

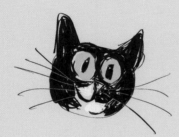

"I feel
peckish."

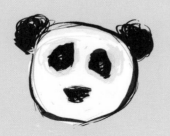

"I'm fucking
livid
actually."

"Panda! me and Teddy have been making lovely pictures with messages of positivity to help everyone!"

"Urgh," says Panda. "They're shit."

"Thank you, Teddy, for the precious gift of your beautiful thoughts and words," said Panda.

"Yeah, they're really uplifting," added the Cat.

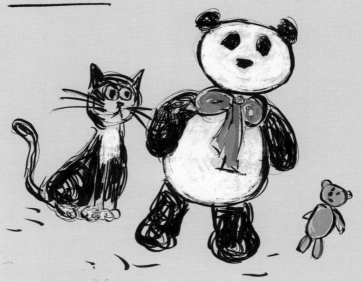

"Cat, I think you should eat that little bastard Teddy...
Just for a laugh."

"Listening is better
than talking,
isn't it, Panda?"

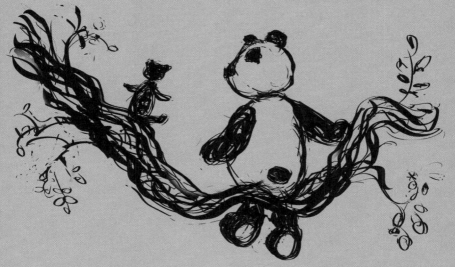

" Shut the fuck up
then, you little twerp."

"I'm reaching for the stars, Panda!"
"Oh, really? I've got a cat's bum on my head."

"I find Panda's words so _soothing_, _calming_ and meaningful," says Teddy.

"What a _fucking_ sycophant."

"I'm living my best life," said Teddy.

"Oh?" said Panda. "Well, go and do it somewhere else, you smug little shite."

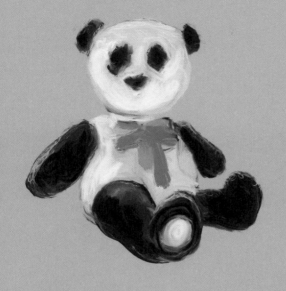

"There really is something inside _so_ strong," says Panda.

"Hurray!"

Gin

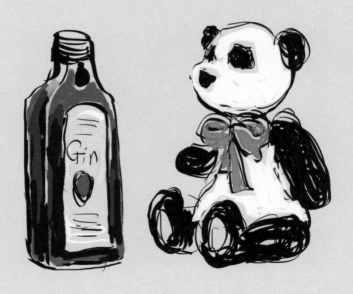

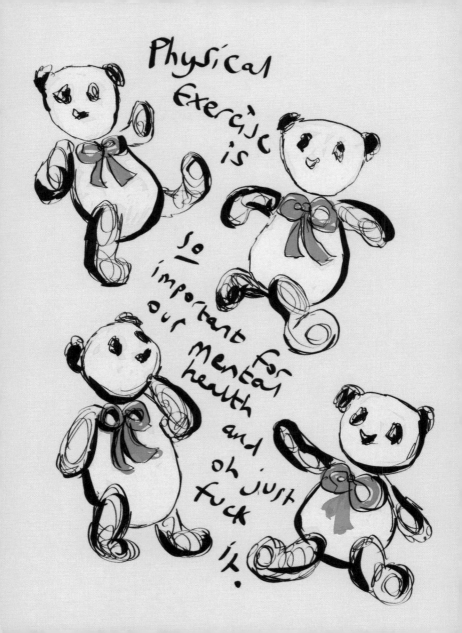

Physical Exercise is

so important for our Mental health and oh just fuck it.

"Sometimes
I feel like
I've
bummed
up
my entire
life,"
thought
Panda.

Hee

Hee

Hee

"You okay, hun?"
asked Panda (but
he was
just taking
the piss).

"Where the
fuck are
we now?"

"Pissing down."

"Surely it's gin time?"

"Just because you're struggling, it doesn't mean that you're failing..."

"But it might do,"

adds Panda.

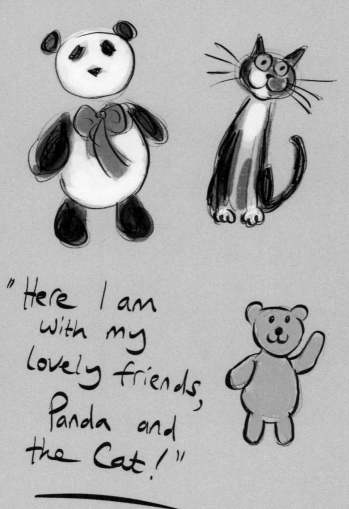

"Here I am with my lovely friends, Panda and the Cat!"

"Bloody Teddy has got himself a cravat...!"

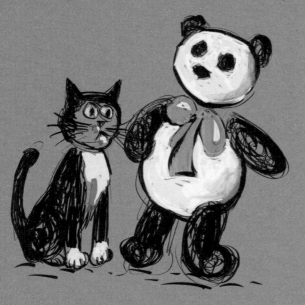

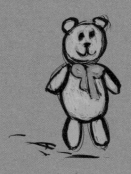

"Sometimes it feels like your friends are such a long way away..."

"...and that can be a relief, frankly."

"Are you really fat like Panda?" asks Teddy. "Why not eat less stuff?"

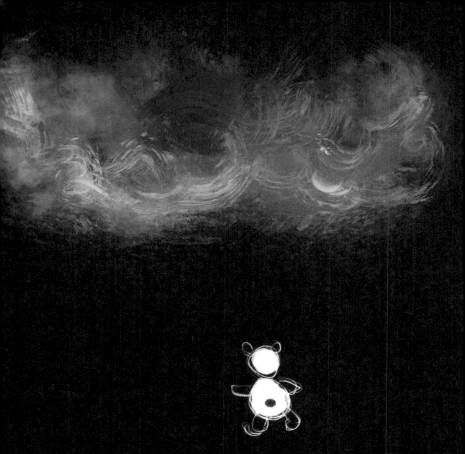

"Another shit storm
on the way."

"Look! It's an empty page! Why's there an empty page...?"

"Stop chatting to that pious little twat and come and play on the swings!" Panda tells the Cat.

oh ffs

"Whew! I'm run off my little feet!" says Teddy. "What do you cats *do* *all* *day*...?"

"Panda..." said the Cat. "Do you ever feel like we're being watched —?"

Oh, bumholes

"Living the
Dream!"

said

Teddy.

"Life can be so beautiful,
so long as you have kindness,
and faith and loveliness and
goodness and niceness and sweetness
and ..."

"Oh somebody make
it fucking stop."

"I've had it with Teddy and his fucking little micro-aggressions."
"Yeah, let's kill him."

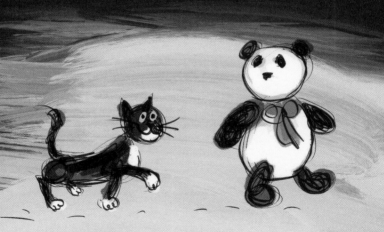

"Nothing beats
Kindness," said
the Cat.

"Gin does,"
said Panda.

"One day we'll be able to get together with all our friends again...

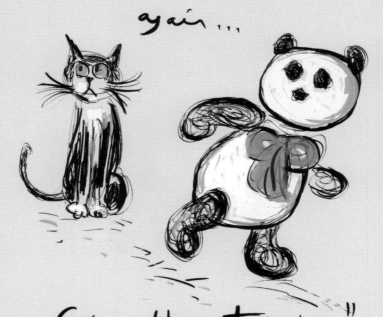

Even the twats."

"Sometimes I think it's the twats I miss the most."

"There goes another name onto the shit-list," said Panda.

Hug
"actually, Cat, you smell a bit bummy."

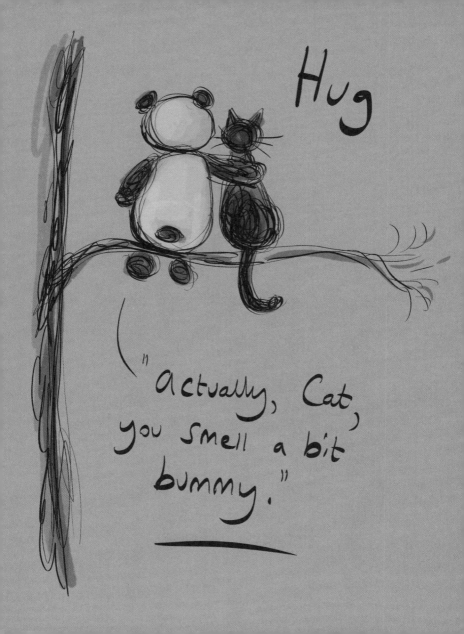

"I'm the Cat!"

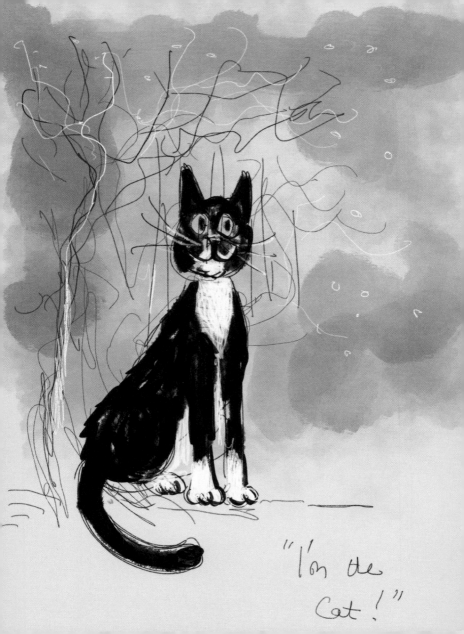

"Not you again!"

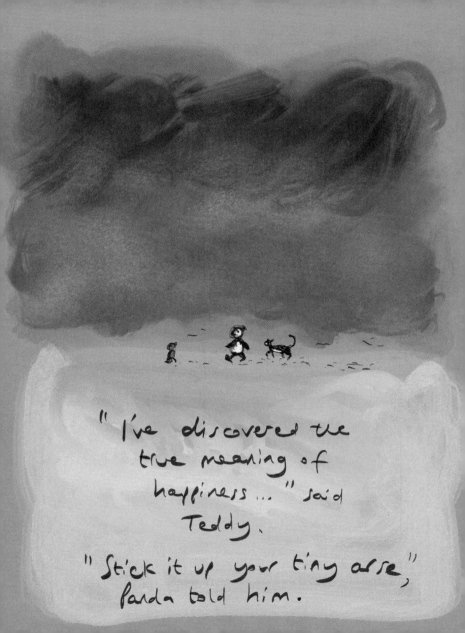

" I've discovered the
true meaning of
happiness ... " said
Teddy.

" Stick it up your tiny arse,"
Panda told him.

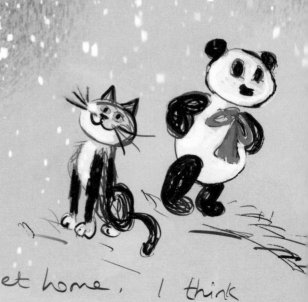

"Let's get home, I think 'Murder she wrote' is on."

"What's even nicer than a cup of tea? a wank."

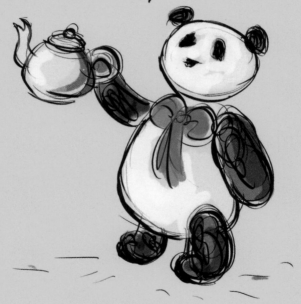

"Do you have any uplifting thoughts to share with everyone in these difficult times, Panda...?"
"No!"

"Be Kind, my arse.
all I want to do is go down the sodding pub."

Teddy and his lovely friends, the Cat + Panda
"Looks like that little fucker Teddy...
...has got a book coming out."

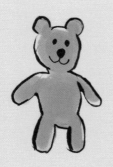

"I'm trying to be as kind as I can."

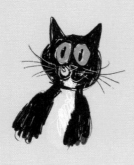

"I'm keeping my bottom clean."

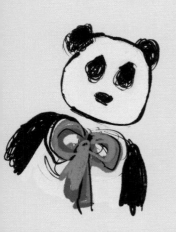

"Mostly I'm telling everyone who annoys me to go and <u>fuck</u> themselves."

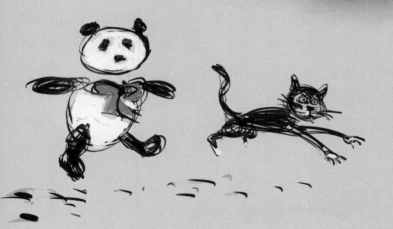

"Best get home before it absolutely <u>pisses</u> down."

"I think it's so important to be kind."
"Do you, Teddy?" asked Panda, just before he pushed him out of the tree.

"It's *so* important to master the art of doing bugger all",

said Panda.

"Sometimes I feel like I haven't achieved much," says Cat.
"You can lick your own doings," Panda points out. "and that's amazing."

"Panda says I'm awesome because I can lick my own asshole!"
"I think Panda has issues, don't you?"

"Help...!"

"Do you know what?
I'm going to just
fanny about all
day tomorrow."

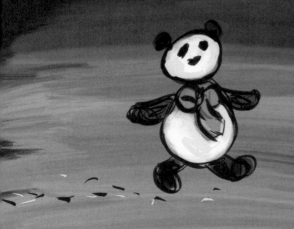

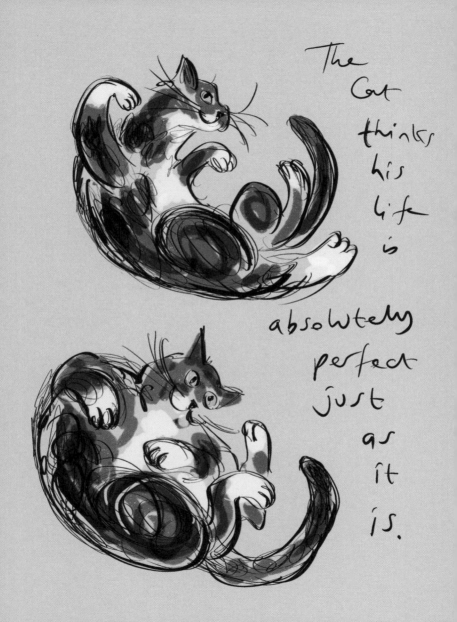

The Cat thinks his life is absolutely perfect just as it is.

"I'm always mindful of being kind."
"Are you indeed, you little twat?"

"I just find that a positive mental attitude can really help with..."
"Oh, do fuck off, Teddy."
"Hee hee hee."

"Dream it.
Wish it.
Do it!"
said Teddy.

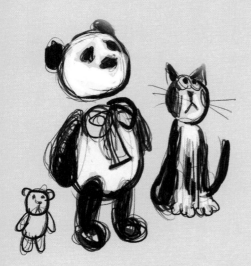

"Fuck it,"
said
Panda.

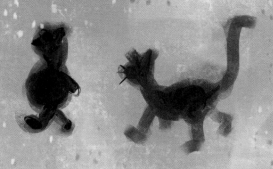

"Is that little creep still following us?"

"Yep."

"Tell me, Panda... did you really like my book?"

Shit, I never read it, thought Panda. "Oh, yes, Teddy –" he said. "I thought it was <u>extraordinary</u>."

"Did you <u>really</u>?" Teddy squealed.

"No, of course not," said Panda. "Extraordinary is what people say when they can't think of any other word,"

"Oh," said Teddy.

"What are you doing, Cat?" asked Teddy.

"I'm licking my asshole, what does it look like?"

"I love you anyway, Panda."

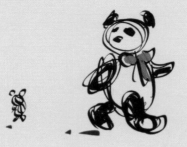

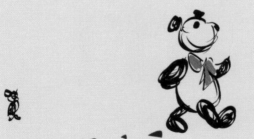

" fuckssake",
said Panda

"Not all heroes wear capes...

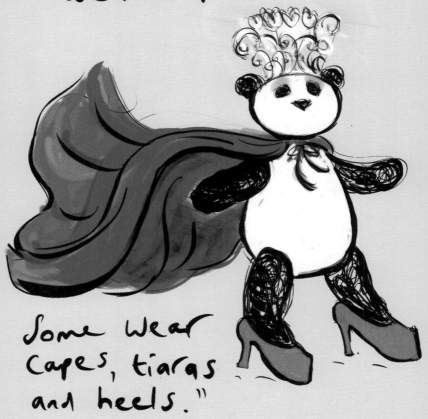

Some wear capes, tiaras and heels."

"Well hello there, bottle of gin. What's that you're saying? You think I should drink all the gin...
... and not give any to my lovely friends—? Oh, okay then."

"aren't you an optimist like me then, Panda?"
Grrrrr
"I think Panda might have turned a little bit bitter!!!"
"He's had a tough life!"
"I can hear you bastards — talking about me!!!"

"You can
kiss my
arse,"

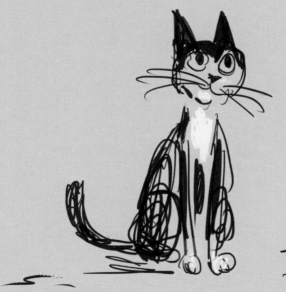

said
the
Cat.

"The sun's come out at last, Panda!"
"It's a bit fucking bright, if you ask me..."

"I was right," says Panda. "Teddy is a fucking user."

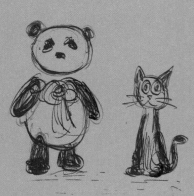

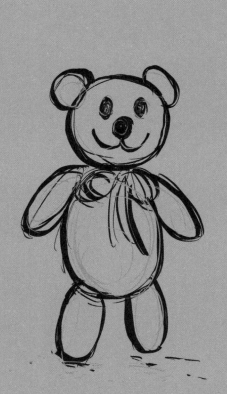

"You're always right, Panda!"
"Though I can be far too trusting and nice sometimes."

"Do you have a specific point, or did you just fancy sitting and *moaning* all day?"

"You have to be the very best you!"
"What the fuck are you talking about, you little gimp?"

"Cat, you've been a lazy arse all day!"
"So...?"

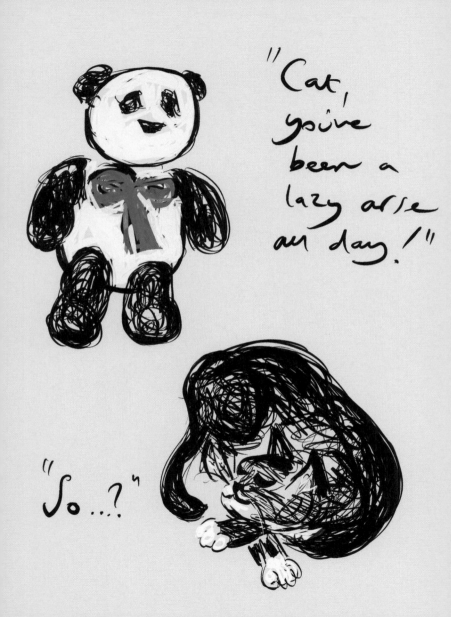

"Don't you ever tell him this, but I sort of miss Teddy when he doesn't play out with us."

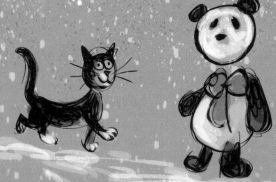

"Where is Teddy, anyway?"

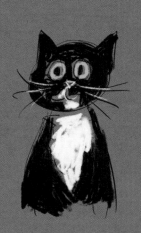

"Book tour, the little shit."

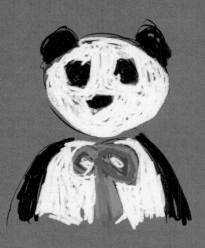

"Is Panda having an off day?"

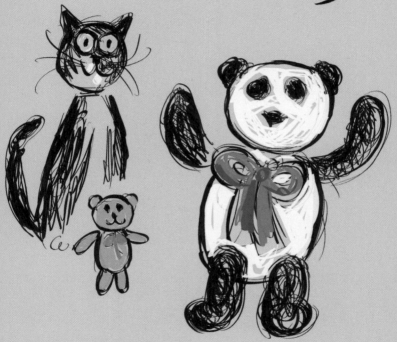

Aaarrrggghh

Teddy Loves You

"Panda! Teddy's come back home!"
""
"Thank you both for being in my special book with me!"
"What the fuck is he on about?"

"You two are the most wonderful friends a little Teddy Bear could ever have!"

"Together we are strong!" Teddy added.

"I love my friends
even when they're
arseholes."
XXX

"I'm so glad that my words and my thoughts have helped you to become better and kinder people," says Teddy.

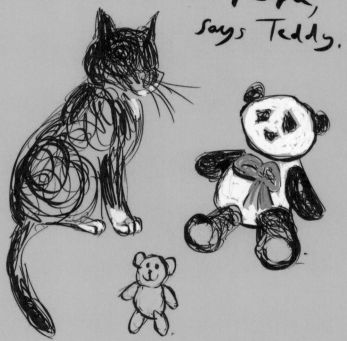

"Oh yes indeed," Panda calls after him. "fuck off now."

"For World Book Day, the Cat, Teddy and myself have chosen to dress up as <u>each other</u>."

"Bugger this —
I'm off," said
Panda.

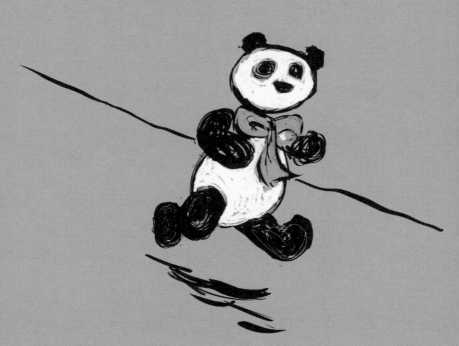

The
End

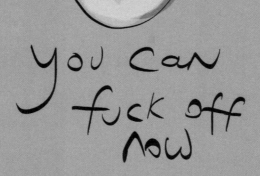

you can
fuck off
now

WTF
now??

Thank Yous

To Jeremy, my Mam and my family. To all the members of fambles. To all our friends. To Piers and to Anna + all at HC. And everyone else who's helped along the way. Love — Paul, Teddy, the Cat and Panda ✳

Paul lives in Manchester
with Jeremy
and everyone in
this book. *